This book was written in Memory of Frances Louise Reed and Alice Fillppetti. For their Love and Faith in the Lord Jesus Christ, and for their motherly devotion and Love to their children. They have made known to me the meaning of the The Greatest Commandment.

Surrounded by beautiful green fields of tall wild grass and flowers of many shapes and colors, a field mouse family lived in their nest hidden deep inside the roots of a large old fig tree.

And God saw everything that He had made, and behold it was very good.

Genesis 1:31

This mouse family had a warm lovely home
which kept them safe from One-
Eyed Blacky, the stray cat,
and kept them warm on
cold rainy days.

The Lord is my Shepherd; I shall not want.

Psalm 23:1

Mama and Papa mouse and their little boy, Toby, had a very special love for each other and all living things. Whether they flew in the air or walked on the ground.

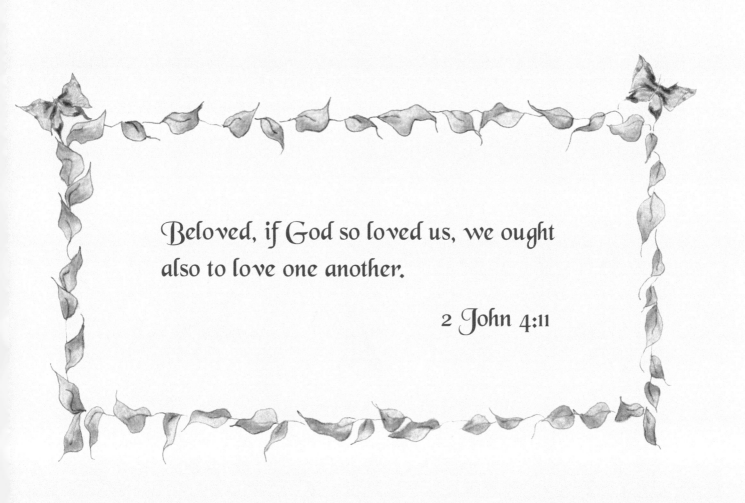

Beloved, if God so loved us, we ought also to love one another.

2 John 4:11

Now, in the early morning, Toby would go out with Papa mouse to learn the things a good mouse needed to know. Papa mouse would teach Toby right from wrong and read to him special words from Heaven above.

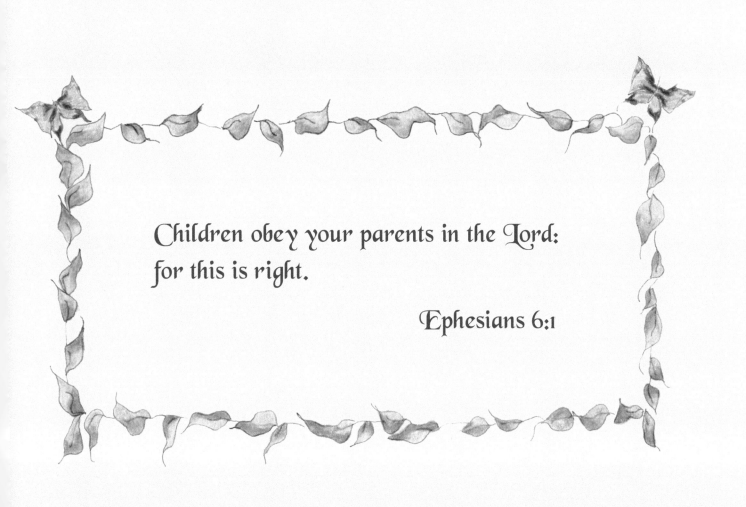

Children obey your parents in the Lord:
for this is right.

Ephesians 6:1

Papa mouse also taught Toby to be kind to others even when others were not so kind to him. He taught Toby to put down his chores to help a friend in need, when their hands were full of weeds. All these things and many more, are what makes a good obedient mouse.

Beloved, let us Love one another for love is of God.

1 John 4:7

Bedtime came early for Toby. Rest and sleep is what a little mouse needs. Tomorrow would be a day full of hopes and good things to see.

The Lord is thy keeper.

Psalm 121:5

The next morning, after a good tasty breakfast of grain and berries, Toby said good-bye to his mother and started on his way across the field to help his father gather food and wood. Down the rocky path he went toward the old farm house where One-Eyed Blacky lived. Quietly Toby peeked around a can to see if Blacky was there, but he was not.

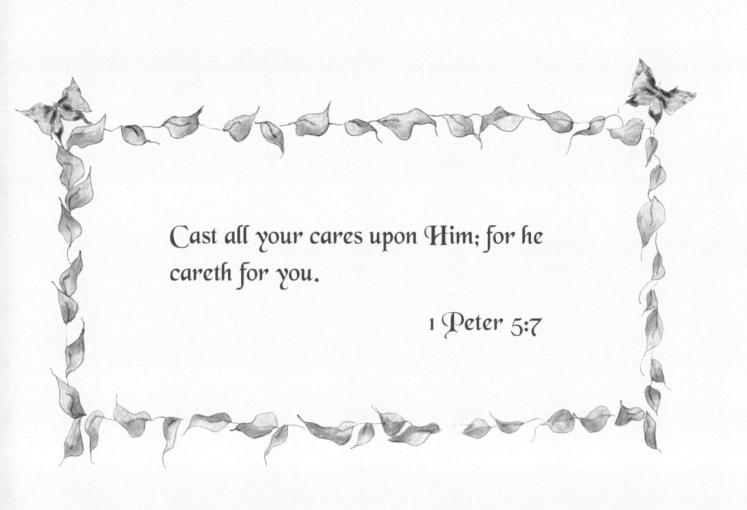

Cast all your cares upon Him; for he careth for you.

1 Peter 5:7

As Toby came to the flower patch, he saw Butterfly, with fear in his eyes, as he fluttered to a quick stop.

Toby asked Butterfly, "What is wrong?" Butterfly said to Toby, "Come quickly! Your father is caught in a trap near the other side of the pond."

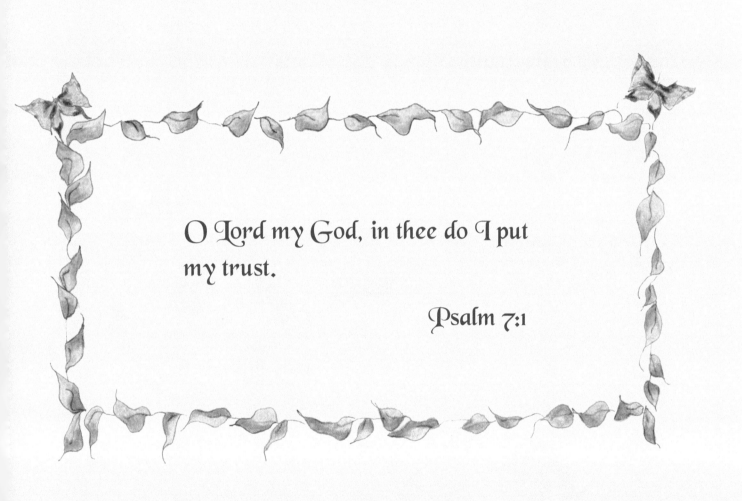

O Lord my God, in thee do I put my trust.

Psalm 7:1

Off ran Toby. Not another word had to be spoken, for Toby knew where One-Eyed Blacky goes to drink water each morning. Butterfly came too, maybe he could be of some help. Fear had come into Toby's heart as he raced along the path to the pond.

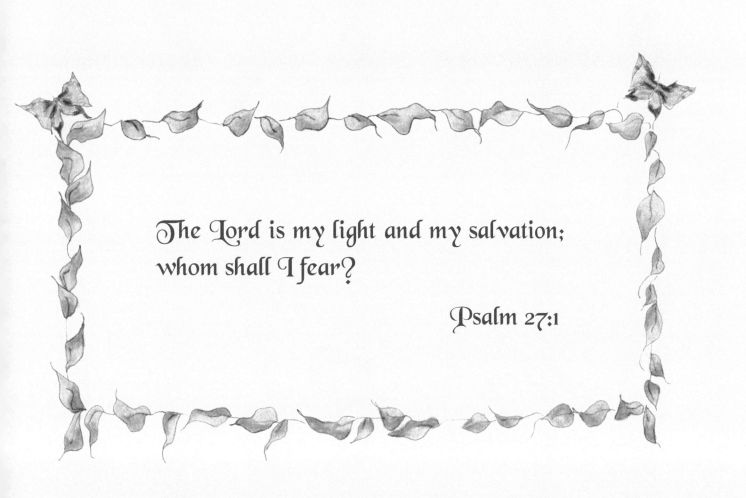

The Lord is my light and my salvation;
whom shall I fear?

Psalm 27:1

As Toby and Butterfly came a few yards from where Papa mouse was, Butterfly spotted One-Eyed Blacky near the edge of the cliff just above the trap. Quickly, Toby dashed down the hill, jumping over rocks, scurrying around trees, stumps, and scattering piles of leaves as he ran. At that same time, Butterfly began to fly circles around One-Eyed Blacky to keep him from seeing Toby.

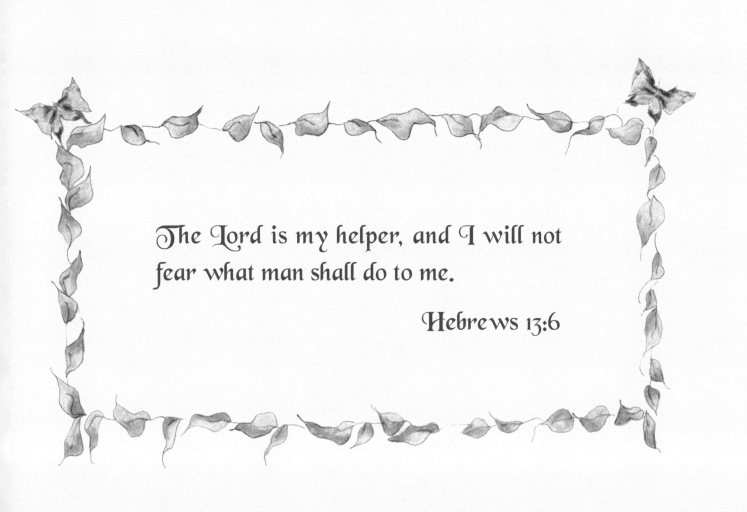

The Lord is my helper, and I will not
fear what man shall do to me.

Hebrews 13:6

Around and around One-Eyed Blacky jumped. Meanwhile, Toby grabbed a twig and opened up the trap just enough to slip his fathers tail out. Together they ran for cover under a tree branch.

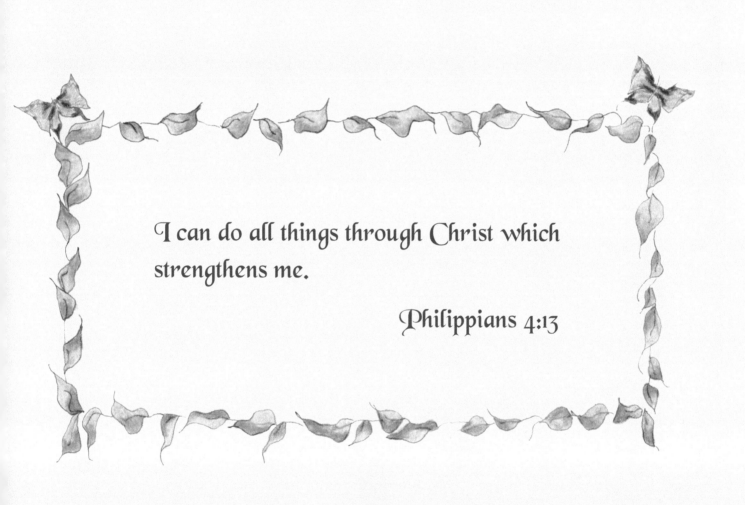

I can do all things through Christ which
strengthens me.

Philippians 4:13

Butterfly still had One-Eyed Blacky jumping in circles. At last Blacky just dropped to the ground tired out, and there he stayed and fell asleep.

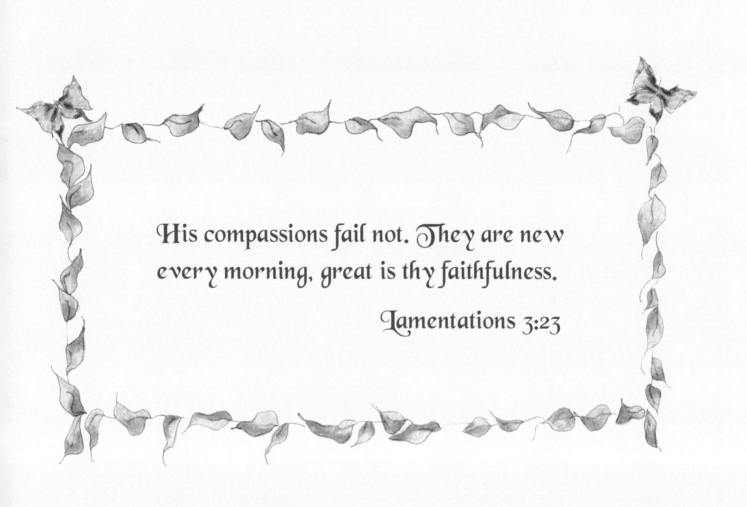

His compassions fail not. They are new
every morning, great is thy faithfulness.

Lamentations 3:23

Toby, Papa mouse, and Butterfly were
three grateful creatures. Not only had
they become good friends, but a great
lesson was taught that day.

Toby, Papa mouse, and
Butterfly would never
forget what happened
that day...Never!

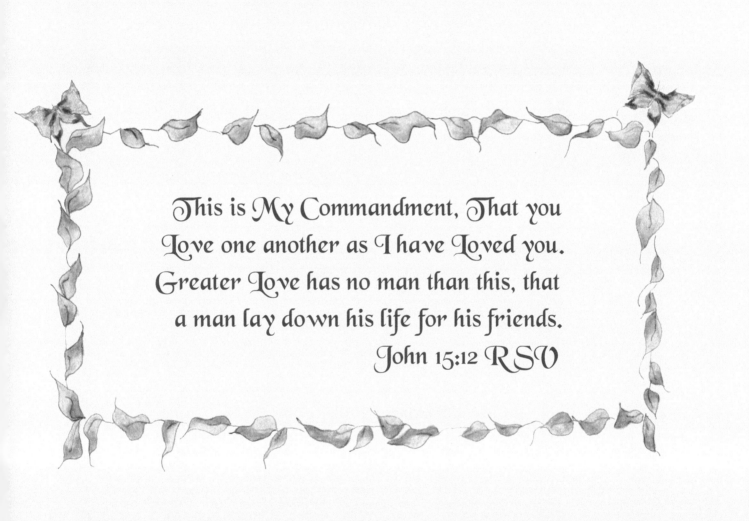

This is My Commandment, That you
Love one another as I have Loved you.
Greater Love has no man than this, that
a man lay down his life for his friends.

John 15:12 RSV

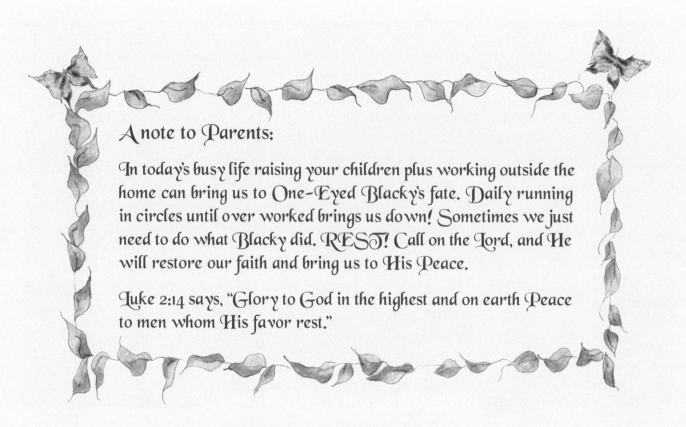

### A note to Parents:

In today's busy life raising your children plus working outside the home can bring us to One-Eyed Blacky's fate. Daily running in circles until over worked brings us down! Sometimes we just need to do what Blacky did. REST! Call on the Lord, and He will restore our faith and bring us to His Peace.

Luke 2:14 says, "Glory to God in the highest and on earth Peace to men whom His favor rest."

Order this book online at www.trafford.com
or email orders@trafford.com

Most Trafford titles are also available at major online book retailers.

 **Trafford** PUBLISHING® www.trafford.com
**North America & international**
toll-free: 844 688 6899 (USA & Canada)
fax: 812 355 4082

Our mission is to efficiently provide the world's finest, most comprehensive book publishing service, enabling every author to experience success. To find out how to publish your book, your way, and have it available worldwide, visit us online at www.trafford.com

Because of the dynamic nature of the Internet, any web addresses or links contained in this book may have changed since publication and may no longer be valid. The views expressed in this work are solely those of the author and do not necessarily reflect the views of the publisher, and the publisher hereby disclaims any responsibility for them.

Any people depicted in stock imagery provided by Getty Images are models, and such images are being used for illustrative purposes only.
Certain stock imagery © Getty Images.

Illustrated by Lynn Reed.

ISBN: 978-1-4251-1955-3 (sc)
ISBN: 978-1-4907-1891-0 (e)

Print information available on the last page.

Trafford rev. 02/19/2021

Printed in the United States
By Bookmasters